Come Along with me on a
Journey
A JOURNEY OF LIFE

JEAN MATTSON

WestBow
PRESS
A DIVISION OF THOMAS NELSON

WestBow Press books may be ordered through booksellers or by contacting:

WestBow Press
A Division of Thomas Nelson
1663 Liberty Drive
Bloomington, IN 47403
www.westbowpress.com
1-(866) 928-1240

Because of the dynamic nature of the Internet, any web addresses or links contained in this book may have changed since publication and may no longer be valid. The views expressed in this work are solely those of the author and do not necessarily reflect the views of the publisher, and the publisher hereby disclaims any responsibility for them.

Any people depicted in stock imagery provided by Thinkstock are models, and such images are being used for illustrative purposes only.

Certain stock imagery © Thinkstock.

ISBN: 978-1-4497-4221-8 (sc)

Library of Congress Control Number: 2012904352

Printed in the United States of America

WestBow Press rev. date: 3/20/2012

To my husband who constantly encourages me to keep writing.

TABLE OF CONTENTS

- INTRODUCTION   xi

I.   MY JOURNEY TO KNOW GOD THROUGH HIS CREATION   1

   1.   The Open Gate   3
   2.   Assurance   4
   3.   You Light My Path   5
   4.   The Closed Gate   6
   5.   A Wall of Protection   7
   6.   God's Protection   8
   7.   What Am I Looking For?   9
   8.   Beautiful Day   10
   9.   Fragile   11
  10.   The Fragrance   12
  11.   Only God Can Make It Happen   13
  12.   The Little Red Blossom   14
  13.   His Eye Is on the Sparrow   15
  14.   Thank You, Jesus   16
  15.   Come Along   17
  16.   Coming Back   18
  17.   Dirty Paws   19
  18.   I Have Decided   20
  19.   Beyond   21
  20.   The Rooster's Crow   22
  21.   Peter   23
  22.   Changing Scenes   25
  23.   The Presence of God   26
  24.   Just for a Moment   27
  25.   Discernment   28
  26.   Break Through   29
  27.   Foundation Stones   30
  28.   The Shadow of His Presence   31

29.	Far Away and Yet So Close	32
30.	Greater Is He	33
31.	My Choice	34
32.	Soar Like an Eagle	35
33.	When I Look Up	36
34.	Walking along the Creek	38
35.	Gentle Intruder	39
36.	Refreshing	40
37.	Four Things	41
38.	The Unoccupied Chair	42

II. MY JOURNEY TO KNOW GOD'S PURPOSES
THROUGH LIFE'S EXPERIENCES   43

1.	God's Love Is Like	45
2.	Complete	46
3.	Peace	47
4.	The Baby's Voice	48
5.	Treasures in Christ Jesus	49
6.	Precious Things	50
7.	Expectation	51
8.	Press On	52
9.	Chosen	53
10.	Step-by-Step	54
11.	Hands... What Meaning They Have!	55
12.	Perfectionism or Love?	57
13.	I Want to Go with You	58
14.	The Light Blue Wool Scarf	59
15.	When Nothing Is Left	61
16.	God's Schedule.... Not Mine	62
17.	God Is Not in a Hurry	63
18.	Waiting	64
19.	He Is Watching	65
20.	Today	66
21.	Today Is a New Page	67
22.	Dear Heavenly Father	68
23.	Accomplishment	69
24.	The Finished Task	70

25. Extended Time 73
26. A Time to Leave 74
27. Someday Soon 75
28. A Window of Time 75
29. Peace in the Time of Storm 76
30. Which Cup? 77

III. MY JOURNEY TO KNOW GOD'S WAYS THROUGH OTHER CULTURES 79

1. Turn Aside 81
2. Unfinished Tasks, Disrupted Lives 82
3. Darkness Cannot Prevail 83
4. Treasures of Darkness 84
5. God Sees 85
6. God Is Good 86
7. His Eyes Are upon You 87
8. Remembering Our Persecuted Family 88
9. Marching 89
10. My Eyes Are on You, Lord 90
11. Come Along With Me on a Trip to China 91
12. Have You Met Jesus 92
13. By Love Serve One Another 93
14. Culture Shock 94
15. Beautiful Canaan Hymns 95
16. Silent Night 96
17. God's Heart for China 97
18. Who Are These? 98
19. Circles 100
20. Contentment 101
21. Reflection 102
22. Lift up Your Voice 103
23. What a Privilege 104
24. Love Is a Universal Language 106
25. Eyes That Cannot See Ears That Cannot Hear 107
26. Special Anniversary 108
27. My Brother's Feet 109

IV.   JOURNEY'S END…THE ULTIMATE GOAL 111

    1. Jesus Will Outshine Them All   113
    2. Just a Foretaste   114
    3. Homesick for Heaven   115
    4. Only One Thing   116
    5. In a Little While   117
    6. The Last Flight   118

LIST OF SONGS   121

RESOURCES   123

INTRODUCTION

Life is a journey; a journey on which every living person is traveling. Life is a gift given to us from God. Every one of us was born into physical life. We have been given a certain amount of time to live on this journey here on earth. Every journey has a destination. The destination of our lives here on earth is determined by whether or not we have spiritual life.

Spiritual life is found in Jesus Christ, God's only begotten Son. Jesus prayed in John 17:3, *And this is life eternal, that they might know You, the only true God, and Jesus Christ whom You have sent.* Jesus said, "I *am the Way, the Truth and the Life, no man comes to the Father except by me.* John 14:6

Come Along with me on a Journey is divided into four parts. My Journey to Know God through His Creation is taken from my journal writings as I wrote about "my morning walks." My Journey to Know God's Purposes is taken from life experiences. My Journey to Know God's Ways is written out of my travels to other cultures. The last section talks about life's final destination. If you have never known Jesus Christ, I pray you will enter into the spiritual journey of knowing Him. Whether you have been "traveling with Jesus" for many years or few, I pray this book will encourage you to keep traveling to your heavenly destiny.

MY JOURNEY TO KNOW GOD THROUGH HIS CREATION

The Open Gate

"Enter His gates with thanksgiving in my heart. "I sang these words as I began my walk down the oak and cedar lined driveway. The beauty of the various green leaves and branches, reaching up toward heaven, reminded me of the beauty of my Creator. As I stepped into the open field, I stood in awe at the vastness of God's creation. The pictures the Lord paints in the cloud formations are numberless. I enjoyed the smell of fresh mown hay along the driveway. At the end of the driveway is an iron gate- the kind my husband and I used when we had cattle in the field. Today, when I reached the gate it was open. Sometimes it is closed.

I think about the "gate of salvation." Today it is open. I want all my loved ones to enter the gate. I want everyone to enter into the "life-gate" that Jesus opened. It is the cross that bridges the gap between every individual and God. I want you who are reading this message, to enter into the "gate of salvation" through faith in the blood of Jesus. He said, *I am the way, the truth, and the life.* John 14:6

Enter in at the strait(narrow) gate; for wide is the gate, and broad is the way, that leads to destruction, and many be which go in there at: Because strait is the gate and narrow is the way, which leads unto life, and few there be that find it. Matthew 7:13-14

Assurance

This morning I went for a walk with Rupert, my daughter's dog, who has come to live with my husband and me. Until now, Rupert has always lived in the city. As we walked through the woods, he was busy sniffing in the grass and leaves, getting acquainted with new territory. When we came to the end of the road that goes through the woods and started through the open field, Rupert kept stopping, turning around to go back, and looking up at me as if to say, " Is it safe? Is it alright for me to go out there?"

This made me think, Do I stop to ask You, Lord, "Is it all right to go out there?" or do I just plow ahead with my own plans not bothering to ask You about them? Finally Rupert kept going forward, walking with me, and not questioning the path any longer. Rupert was assured that everything was all right.

Psalm 112 has wonderful promises of assurance for those who trust in the Lord. vs. 4- *Unto the upright there arises light in the darkness.* Verses 6-8 *Surely he shall never be shaken. He shall not be afraid of evil tidings: His heart is steadfast, trusting in the Lord. His heart is established, He shall not be afraid.*

Similarly, Psalm 91:3 says, *Surely He shall deliver you from the snare of the fowler and from the perilous pestilence.*

You Light My Path

It was early this morning, just at daybreak, when Rupert and I set out on our walk. I began to think of all kinds of animals that might be out there-animals that lurk in the darkness. These include wolves, panthers, wild boars, and skunks. Then I began to think of the promises of God's protection. *Whenever I am afraid, I will trust in You.* Psalm 56:3 At that early hour, when I looked in the distance, the gate at the end of the field seemed dark and formidable; however, the most amazing thing happened. The closer we came to the gate, the brighter the light of the morning became. When we arrived at the gate it was not dark at all, but light.

I am so glad, Lord Jesus, that You came to give me light. You shine in my heart. You are the light that shines in a dark place until the day dawns. You make darkness light before me. Your Word is a lamp unto my feet and a light unto my path. You will light my darkness. I can go forward in this dark world, walking in the light of your Word, assured each step I take you will light my path.

The Closed Gate

It was later in the day when Rupert and I started our walk down the driveway. As we came around the corner I noticed the gate was closed. It is almost always open. I thought, with some hesitancy, about opening it. I kept going. I noticed three animals rushing by on the road outside the gate. They were about the size of a skunk or an armadillo; however, they didn't have the markings of a skunk and were much too quick to be armadillos. Their noses were pointed to the ground and they didn't notice me. Rupert didn't see the animals.

I quickly turned around and started running with Rupert. We ran all the way to the corner. I looked back; none of the animals had followed us. I wonder, "were those wild pigs that I saw?"

The gate was closed for a purpose. Inside the gate was protection. Sometimes the Lord has an open door for us to go through, and other times a door is closed. If things do not seem to work out at the time, or way, we would like them to; perhaps God is keeping that door closed for a reason. He is able to see everything that is happening and desires the best for his children. I don't want to wander outside the "gate of God's protection." When He has a closed door it is for my benefit.

A Wall of Protection

This morning the fog was extremely thick. It was like a huge wall coming down from the sky to the ground. It surrounded me on all sides. I could not even see the headlights of the cars that I heard going by on the road beyond the gate; yet, in the place where I was walking I could clearly see the path.

God led the children of Israel by a pillar of cloud. That pillar of cloud stood like a wall between them and the Egyptians. That cloud contained God's presence. It was darkness to the enemy, but gave light by night to the Israelites, so that one could not come near to the other. God could see through the pillar of cloud and troubled the Egyptians. In times of darkness, God will lead me in the ways that I cannot see now. His hand on me in the darkness is protection from the enemy.

God's Protection

This morning, as I began my walk, Rupert, my dog, lagged behind. I called him several times; conversely, on the way back he ran as fast as he could! All I could see was a ball of fur. He was over half way home before he stopped to see if I was coming. With Rupert at my side, I felt free from danger; his sharp bark warned any predator. Now I was alone. I felt helpless.

So it is spiritually: "Without You, Lord, I am completely helpless. I am completely vulnerable to the attack of the enemy. But your truth counter-attacks the enemy's lies. By faith, I believe You shield me from his fiery darts. I cry out to You, save me, O my God. You come to my rescue. You are my Savior, my Defense."

What Am I Looking For?

When I walked through the woods this morning, I noticed a large clearing; I could see for a long distance. No wild animal would be able to sneak up on me. I felt safe. I kept walking until I reached the gate. Looking back at the field, I pictured in my mind, a panther bounding across the field toward me. Could I hide between the huge hay bales? Not really.

I thought about the Lord's protection. I noticed a little leaf falling to the ground. I remembered the Lord says He sees even the little sparrow that falls to the ground.

Matthew 10:29-31 *Are not two sparrows sold for a copper coin? And not one of them falls to the ground apart from your Father's will. But the very hairs of your head are all numbered. Do not fear therefore; you are of more value than many sparrows.*

Beautiful Day

I picked wild flowers along the driveway on my morning walks this week. I enjoy the various kinds of flowers and tried to pick a different kind of bouquet to bring home each day. I noticed some dainty, purple flowers blooming in the tall grass, in the corner of the field near the road.

Our daughter, Darlene, is coming to visit my husband and me today. I wanted to pick these special flowers for Darlene. Would it be wise to walk in the tall grass? Snakes may be crawling there. My husband stopped on his way to work. He picked the flowers for me. What a wonderful way to start the day. What a beautiful day!

I visualized the children coming to see Jesus. They were bringing flowers to the One who created both them and the flowers. Jesus took the children up in His arms and blessed them. I thought about the beauty of the Lord and sang, "O worship the Lord in the beauty of holiness." That is what is beautiful, His holiness. Psalm 149:4 says that He *will beautify the humble with salvation.* Psalm 90:17 says, *let the beauty of the LORD our God be upon u*s.

Fragile

Today I saw the beauty of the flowers. I picked Indian paintbrushes, a little yellow flower, and a fragile, purple flower. When I arrived back at the house I found a crystal vase, filled it with cool water, and gently placed the flowers in it. I set the bouquet on the dining room table where I could enjoy the flowers every time I sat down to a meal. The next morning the Indian paintbrushes were still bright orange, the yellow flower was a little droopy, but the fragile, purple flower showed no signs of life.

Life is like the fragile flower; it is here one day and gone the next. The glory of man is like the flower that fades. The beauty and intricate design of the flowers reminds me of God's mercy and love. God puts so much delicacy and beauty into the design of fragile flowers that soon disappear; we are much more important to Him. I need not be anxious. I need to trust in His provision for me.

So why do you worry about clothing? Consider the lilies of the field, how they grow: they neither toil nor spin; and yet I say to you that even Solomon in all his glory was not arrayed like one of these. Now if God so clothes the grass of the field, which today is, and tomorrow is thrown into the oven, will He not much more clothe you, O you of little faith? Matthew 6:28-30

The Fragrance

The air and gentle breeze was refreshing today. The temperature was in the low 60's. It was so good to be walking with You again, Lord, in the cool of the day. I began to sing: "You are worthy, Lord". Looking over the mown field, I saw the flowers that bloomed abundantly are now being mowed down.

I am reminded of your Word that says, *because All flesh is as grass, And all the glory of man as the flower of the grass The grass withers, And its flower falls away, but the word of the LORD endures forever.* I Peter1:24-25. . May I ever glorify You, Lord, and not rely on the glory of man.

On the way home, just before the path enters the woods, I saw white, delicate flowers blooming at the end of the field. The mower has not touched them. They were gently swaying in the wind. Blow on me Holy Spirit, wind of God, bring forth the fragrance of Jesus.

Only God Can Make It Happen

I stepped unto the deck and noticed the rapid growth of the Aloe plant. Taking a closer look, I saw three buds on the plant. I didn't know Aloe plants had blossoms. I wondered, "What color will the blossoms be?"

I am reminded of an incident when a small child opened up the bud of a rose, expecting to see a beautiful flower. The flower was not fully developed; instead of a beautiful rose, she found only separate rose petals. Only God can cause the buds of a plant to open into beautiful blossoms.

If the eggshell is broken open before the baby bird or chick is fully developed, only death is evident. Only God can cause the baby to wait until it is fully developed to crack open the shell.

Sometimes in life one encounters trials that last so long. Perhaps one tries to "help God out" in some way. Things get really messed up. Last night I saw the most beautiful rainbow. It reminded me that God always keeps His promises! Only He can make it happen.

The Little Red Blossom

I am utterly amazed at the many ways God, through His creation, illustrates the truth of His gospel. My son and his family gave me a beautiful arrangement of flowers in a flower pot appropriate to be outside. I enjoyed the flowers when I went outside every day. Then one weekend my husband and I were visiting away from home. The sun became hotter and the flowers became drier from lack of water. Some of them died. I watered the remaining flowers and hoped for the best. Eventually all of the flowers dried up. I felt bad and put the flowerpot in back of the house out of view.

Several days ago, when I was going into the house from my worship time, I glanced to the left of the ramp and noticed a bright red blossom. What was so unusual about that red blossom? The plant which had died was revived. Unknown to me, my other son placed the flower pot where it was shaded from the heat of the sun. Lots of bright green foliage started growing in the flowerpot but the pretty red blossom especially stood out.

The revived blossom reminds me of the words in the Scripture, *And you He made alive, who were dead in trespasses and sins.* Ephesians 2:1 the red reminds me of Jesus' blood that was shed for our sins, making it possible for us to have new life. The revived plant also reminds me we must never become discouraged and never give up when it looks like all hope is dying. *Hope in God, for I shall yet praise Him for the help of His countenance.* Psalm 42:5

His Eye Is on the Sparrow

It was 60 degrees this morning and the breeze blowing in my hair felt refreshing. I walked through the woods and looked up into the sky. Everywhere I saw little patches of blue; wisps of dark clouds were moving swiftly through the sky. I kept watching. The scene kept changing, from less blue sky to more grey clouds. The brightness of the sunlight edged around the clouds to the east. I kept walking, thinking about changes. Someday I will take my last walk in the woods and through the field. I began to feel a little sad. Then the words of a song came to my mind.

I sing because I'm happy
I sing because I'm free
For His eye is on the sparrow
And I know He watches over me

Thank You, Jesus

Thank You, Jesus, Thank You Lord
Thank You for salvation
So precious and so free.
Yet, it cost You more than I can comprehend
To die on the cross to set me free.

Thank You for Your grace,
Thank You for Your healing power,
And thank You for every circumstance
You allow in my life today.
Thank You for teaching me Your way.

Come Along

This morning was a beautiful sunny day, although the temperature was only 36 degrees. I started down the driveway for my walk with my dog, Rupert. I began singing and praising the Lord and then noticed Rupert was nowhere in sight. I called him several times. "Come along, come along, Rupert!" Finally, he came running to catch up with me. I nearly stumbled on a loose stone and noticed many loose stones on the path. When I walked home the wind was blowing in my face. I began singing:

Come along with me on the narrow way
On the way of truth and light
Let us go together in the heavenly way
To the place where there is no more night.
Though the way seems hard and long
Though the wind of adversity blow
Do not turn back, but know,
Our Savior is strong;
And He will carry you through.
Come along with me,
My brother and my sister.

Coming Back

This morning Rupert wanted to wander off the chosen path. He didn't know there might be snakes or other dangers he might encounter. I began singing and praising the Lord. After I had been singing and we had walked awhile, Rupert stopped and looked right at me with eyes that said, "I love you." I stopped and petted him a little; then we started walking again.

We are so prone to wander off God's path to places where we are vulnerable to the enemy of our souls. Then it is time to stop and remember how much Jesus loves us and start walking with him again. I am reminded of a song that I learned as a child.

I am so glad that our Father in heaven tells of His love in the book He has given
Wonderful things in the Bible I see, this is the dearest that Jesus loves me
Though I forget Him and wander away, still He does love me wherever I stray
Back to His dear loving arms would I flee, when I remember that Jesus loves me.
It is the love of Jesus that can bring an erring child back to Him. Hosea has a wonderful promise for backsliding Israel. *I will heal their backsliding; I will love them freely; for mine anger is turned away from him.* Hosea 14:4

Dirty Paws

Last night I cleaned my walking shoes; I wanted to walk where they would not get so dirty again. The gravel and sandy parts of the driveway were wet from the rain. Because of the heavy dew, the grassy part was also wet. I chose, as much as possible, to walk on the grassy part. When there was no grassy part I tried to find smooth rocks to walk on. It worked. My shoes only picked up a thin layer of dirt that was easy to wipe off. I noticed Rupert's paws were becoming more and more soiled. He gathered dirt from each step he took. When we arrived back at the house I took a towel and tried to clean Rupert's paws. He growled and snapped at me.

What a lesson Rupert taught me this morning. How do I treat the people the Lord uses to confront me when he wants to clean up my "walk?"Do I get angry about it; perhaps "biting and devouring" those around me with the words that I speak when they try to correct me? Do I get protective about my sinful habits and make excuses? Rupert was very protective of his dirty paws. The Lord will never force me to clean up my walk. I can choose to let Him cleanse me by taking heed to His Word, or I can choose to be like Rupert and keep my feet dirty. Jesus washed His disciple's feet. We are to wash one another's feet and pray for one another's walk.

I Have Decided

This morning was delightfully cool, nearly cold; however, walking kept me warm. Rupert wanted to turn around and go back until he must have realized we were going to keep walking until we came to the gate. We even went farther on the road.

I began to think what the Scripture says about "turning back." When Lot's wife looked back she became a pillar of salt. When the Israelites looked at the enemy, instead of at God's promises; they wanted to turn back from going into the Promised Land. The prophet of God was slain by a lion because he disobeyed God, and turned back, when God had told him not to go back the same way.

Jesus said, *"No one, having put his hand to the plough and looking back, is fit for the kingdom of God."* Luke 9:62. The rich young ruler sorrowfully turned away from Jesus.

There is a song that greatly impresses me.

I have decided to follow Jesus
No turning back, no turning back.
Though none go with me, yet still I'll follow
No turning back, no turning back.

(Continued next page)

In all your disappointments, don't turn back,
don't turn back.

Don't turn away from the Lord who loved you so;
He promised never to forsake you, don't turn back.
Don't turn away from His love;
He will see you through.
With outstretched arms He is calling you,
"Don't turn back, I am praying for you."

Beyond

Beyond my circumstances
Beyond my pain
There is Jesus, God's dear Son
The victory He has won.
Right there in the midst of the storm,
He sets me free from all alarm.
Open my eyes, Lord,
That I may see your face;
Open my ears, that I may hear your voice.
Open my lips, to praise you at all times.

The Rooster's Crow

Today I heard the rooster crow. It reminded me how Peter was warned that he would deny Christ three times before the rooster crowed. Later, when I drove to the store, I saw five roosters walking down the road. They were unaware that they might be hit by an automobile. I need to be alert, awake, and pay attention to God's warnings; then I will not deny Him.

Also, I heard the owls hoot. Were they saying, "Who, Who, Who is greater than the God who created us?" Were they praising Him as all creation praises His Name?

Praise the LORD from the earth, You great sea creatures and all the depths; Fire and hail, snow, and clouds'; Stormy wind, fulfilling his word; Mountains and all hills; Fruitful trees, and all cedars; Beasts, and all cattle; Creeping things and flying fowl. Psalms 148:7-10

Peter

Peter was a man of action
His zeal for Jesus could not be hidden.
He stepped right outside the boat
Ready to walk on water.
When Peter began to sink
Jesus stretched out His hand.
With eyes on Jesus, Peter could stand.

When on the mountaintop with Jesus
Peter feared, not knowing what to do.
"It's time to build a tent," he said.
But the Father spoke in words so true-
"Take time to listen to my Son,
For He will tell you what to do."

When soldiers came to take Jesus,
Peter quickly was at His side.
He wielded his sword, cut off the servant's ear.
But Jesus said, "Put down your sword,
Ten thousand angels I could call,
But now is the time to do the Father's will."

When Jesus had raised from the dead
His presence to His disciples He did show.
Peter thought, "There must be something I can do
To show my love to Him is true."
The fish and bread Jesus did provide.
A new mandate Peter heard Him say,
"Feed my sheep, feed my lambs."

(continued next page)

How much like Peter in myself I see-
A desire with all my heart to serve
The One who gave His life for me.
When enthralled with His sweet presence
A million thoughts come rushing to my mind
Of all the things that I could do.
It is not time for me to "build a tent" but
Listen quietly to my Savior's voice,
To know where He would have me sent.

When faced with the enemy of my soul
How quickly I take up the sword of self-defense.
I cannot fight the battle with this carnal flesh-
The Lord is my Deliverer, in His power the battle lays,
When in submission to His will the victory is won.

When I ponder on all that I can do for you
Lord, help me to hear voice,
"Feed my sheep; feed my lambs."
By obeying Your will I can surely show
The degree of my love for You.
I'll feed Your sheep; I'll feed Your lambs,
By Your grace Your mandate I will obey.

Changing Scenes

This morning I noticed many changing scenes in the sky. White billowy clouds in the Southwest turned to grey, rolling, and dark clouds in the West. I thought of the words in Malachi 3:6, *For I am the LORD, I do not change; Therefore you are not consumed, O sons of Jacob.* Because He changes not, we are not consumed.

Lamentations 3:22 says, *Through the LORD's mercies we are not consumed, Because His compassions fail not.* Numbers 23:19 says, *God is not a man, that He should lie, nor a son of man, that He should repent. Has He said, and will He not do? Or has He spoken, and will He not make it good?* We can depend upon the LORD.

My God can do anything but fail,
My God can do what He says He will do,
His promises are all true.
My God will bring you through.

My God can do anything, anytime, anywhere,
My God can do anything but fail.

The Presence of God

This morning the sun was shining very brightly upon the dew making it glisten. The grass in the field had a white appearance. I began singing "Shine on me, Holy Spirit, shine in my soul making me whole. Dispel all doubt and darkness. Discover every goal and passion. Oh, Holy Spirit shine in my soul, conform me to the image of the brightness of Christ".

I saw a thick cloud of fog above the earth. I thought about Moses and the children of Israel. Moses entered into the cloud, into the presence of God, into the secret place. I want to enter into that secret place where I may discover the very nature of God, the place of worship.

Now the LORD descended in the cloud and stood with him there, and proclaimed the name of the LORD. And the LORD passed before him and proclaimed, "The LORD, the LORD God, merciful and gracious, longsuffering, and abounding in goodness and truth, keeping mercy for thousands, forgiving iniquity and transgression and sin, by no means clearing the guilty, visiting the iniquity of the fathers upon the children and the children's children to the third and the fourth generation." Exodus 34:5-7

Just for a Moment

The sun burst forth, with sparkling bright rays through the openings in the trees, reminding me of Your brightness, Jesus. Hebrews 1:3 says, *who being the brightness of His glory and the express image of His person.* My finite mind cannot comprehend how glorious you are! As I walked farther toward the road, the sun was suddenly hidden behind the trees. For a moment, I could not see the brightness of the sun.

In Isaiah 54:7, 8 we read, *For a mere moment I have forsaken you, But with great mercies I will gather you. With a little wrath I hid My face from you for a moment; But with everlasting kindness I will have mercy on you, says the LORD, your Redeemer.* That is God's promise to Israel; yet, it shows God's character concerning all of His children.

Help me always to remember, although "for a moment" I do not feel your presence, your loving kindness and mercy is everlasting. What a wonderful promise to cling to when our pathway is scattered with clouds of doubt and despair.

Discernment

This morning when I came to the part of the driveway that leaves the woods and goes through the open field, suddenly I saw a large spider's web hanging from the tree branches. It spread nearly to the middle of the driveway. The spider, that was still spinning the web, was almost in front of my nose. A ray of sunlight shining on the web enabled me to see the web and the spider.

On my way back home from the gate, I knew about the spider web so I walked to the other side of the driveway to avoid it. As I glanced to my right, I noticed the spider web had been getting bigger than when I first saw it. Because there was no ray of sunlight shinning on the web, I could have easily walked right into it.

The Lord was drawing me a picture from His awesome creation. The spider web could only be seen when the sun shinned upon it. It is only when the Son of God is shining His Light upon our way that we can discern the "web or snare" that Satan would have us walk right into. God's Word is light for our path. We need to keep our eyes on Jesus who is the Light of the world so we do not become ensnared by Satan's lies.

Break Through

As I stepped outside the door, I could see wisps of spider web makings here and there from tree to tree. The sunlight was not shining directly upon the trees surrounding my pathway; therefore, I knew I might encounter running into an unseen web. Yet, there was no way around. I quickly walked to my destination. I could feel the cobweb in my hair. I brushed it off, along with the spider that fell to the ground. It was worth breaking through the spider woven path to come to the place where I could enjoy the beautiful picture that God was painting for me.

The sky was filled with white billowy clouds; I had to peer with eyes partly closed at their brightness. I sat in my "outdoor cathedral" and enjoyed the stillness. Suddenly, the sunrays broke through the clouds; no spider webs could be hidden from the sun's brilliance.

Sometimes we see a trial coming and we would like to go some other way; however, the Lord knows we must go through that trial to be able to experience the place of beautiful fellowship with Him. Other times we encounter unseen, unexpected trials.

Our Heavenly Father knows just what we need to break through in our lives; to walk in close fellowship with Him- perhaps it is pride, fear, cares of this world, and sorrow. These are all enemies of our soul. In I Chronicles14:11, King David describes God's victory over his enemies, *"God has broken through my enemies by my hand like a breakthrough of water.* "Jesus has broken the power of every enemy of our soul. He has come to set the captive free.

Foundation Stones

This morning I began to praise You, Lord, and asked You to speak to me. I noticed some loose pebbles in the driveway. Then I began to focus on singing praise to You. It was very still this morning with no breeze and no country sounds. I prayed, "Lord, you spoke to Elijah in the stillness, speak to me in the stillness." Then I noticed the stones. They are loose from the foundation.

I was reminded the words of a song:

How firm a foundation you saints of the Lord,

Is laid for your faith in His excellent Word.

What more can He say than to you He has said,

To you, who for refuge to Jesus have fled.

The words to the song are so beautiful! Those who put their faith in Jesus Christ have a sure foundation that cannot be shaken.

Hebrews 6:18-19 says, *that by two immutable things, in which it is impossible for God to lie, we might have strong consolation, who have fled for refuge to lay hold of the hope set before us. This hope we have as an anchor of the soul , both sure and steadfast, and which enters the Presence behind the veil.* Our foundation stands sure; we cannot be shaken loose from Jesus.

Hebrew 12:27 talks about, *those things that are being shaken as of things that are made, that the things which cannot be shaken may remain.*

II Thessalonians 2:2 says *not to be soon shaken in mind or troubled.*

The Shadow of His Presence

This morning everything was completely still - not a rustle of the leaves, nor chirping of the birds was heard; no cattle were seen moving about in the field as I started my morning walk through the woods and field.

As I turned the corner in the pathway, I noticed my shadow. A shadow is absolutely silent, yet, truly present. Lord, when I feel that You are silent, may I remember that You are truly present. In Psalm 23:4 David says, *Yea, though I walk through the valley of the shadow of death, I will fear no evil; For you are with me.*

Many other Psalms refer to the shadow of God's wings.

Psalm 17:8 says, *Hide me under the shadow of Your wings.*

Psalm 36:7 How precious is Your loving-kindness, O God! Therefore the children of men put their trust under the shadow of Your wings.

Psalm 57:1 And in the shadow of Your wings, I will make my refuge

Psalm 63:7 Therefore in the shadow of Your wings I will rejoice

Far Away and Yet So Close

What a beautiful spring day! The temperature was 60 degrees; the sun was shining brightly. The country air was refreshing. As I walked through the woods I heard the chirping of a bird; however, thick branches and leaves hid the bird from my view. I continued my walk into the field. I heard the far away sound of an airplane; I looked up into the cloudless, blue sky, but the airplane was out of sight. I am glad, Lord, though you are far away, I am in your sight.

Lord, You are close to me, in every breath I take

You are my very life.

You are as close as I open up my heart to You

And let You come inside.

Lord, You are close enough

For me to hear Your gentle whisper,

Guiding me along life's way.

You are close enough to see each teardrop,

Close enough to keep my feet from falling.

Now to Him who is able to keep you from stumbling, and to present you faultless Before the presence of his glory with exceeding joy, To God our Savior, Who alone is wise, Be glory and majesty, Dominion and power, both now and forever. Amen. Jude 24-25

Greater Is He

Greater is He that is in me than he that is in the world
Greater is His love in me than the love that is in the world
Greater is His joy in me than the joy that is in the world
Greater is His power in me than the power that is in the world.

Greater is Your love poured out in my life,
Greater than any sacrifice that I could ever make,
Greater than any persecution I could endure,
Greater is Your love in me than the love that is in the world.

Greater is Your joy to those who obey Your voice,
Greater is Your joy to those who walk in truth
Setting free from words that would enslave,
Greater is Your joy in me than the joy that is in the world.

Greater is Your power to do mighty works,
Greater is Your power to those who believe,
Greater to do the works You ordained,
Greater is Your power in me than the power that is in the world.

My God is greater than anything I have to deal with today.
He is the Mighty Conqueror who lives within my soul.

My Choice

A few days ago, when I went on my morning walk, the mosquitoes tried to get in between my glasses and into my eyes. They bit my hands and tried to fly into my mouth, when I was singing praises to my Lord. This was very disturbing and I thought, "I cannot go on any more walks because the mosquitoes are so bad!" This morning it occurred to me that I have insect repellant that I can put on my face, arms, neck, and feet. I wore long pants and long sleeves. Praise the Lord, the repellant did the job. A mosquito only came near my face one time.

I could have the victory over the mosquitoes; I may have the victory over the enemy of my soul. What repels Satan? The blood of Jesus.does. I am covered by the blood of Jesus. By the shield of faith, I can quench the fiery darts of the enemy.

I have a choice; I may stay in the house, (and not go on any more walks), or I may put the repellant on and enjoy those special walks out in God's creation, in fellowship with Him. I may decide not to go out into the world, seeking the lost, (because there are too many enemies out there), or I may take up the shield of faith, put on the shoes of the preparation of the gospel of peace, and go with Jesus wherever He leads.

Soar Like an Eagle

This morning I saw a beautiful eagle soaring far up in the sky. Father, you spoke to me and said, " How can you soar like an eagle when you have an independent spirit?" Soaring cannot be accomplished by self-effort. Instead, we must recognize, by faith, we are seated in heavenly places with Christ Jesus. *But God who is rich in mercy, because of his great love with which He loved us, even when we were dead in trespasses, made us alive together with Christ, (by grace you have been saved) and raised us up together; and made us sit together in the heavenly places in Christ Jesus.* Ephesians 2:4-6

To soar like the eagle, we must, by faith, take our place seated with Christ far above all the principalities and powers of darkness. We must realize that, "In Christ,"we have already defeated the enemy of our souls.

To soar with Christ, we must learn to wait upon Him.

Isaiah 40:31 says, *But those who wait on the LORD shall renew their strength; They shall mount up with wings like eagles, They shall run and not be weary, They shall walk and not faint.*

When I Look Up

I was so glad to see the 72 degrees temperature this morning. I sat down in my lawn chair and began to sing praises to my Heavenly Father. When I looked down I saw the barren ground and the withered leaves on my hydrangea plant (due to the 110 degree weather). When I looked up I saw the beauty of the green trees, as the light of the sun shone through them. The rustling of the leaves in the light breeze reminded me that there is life. Indeed, Lord, there is life in You. You led the children of Israel through the barren wilderness. You provided for their needs.

I took a walk through my son's tomato patch. The vines are spreading upon the fence; they are filled with blossoms. More small tomatoes are appearing every day. My son faithfully waters these plants every night. Thank You, Lord, for turning my thoughts upward, toward You Who are the Source of Life.

When I look down upon the trials of this life I could easily be overcome with sadness, weariness, and hopelessness; but when I look up to You, Lord, I am encouraged and rejoice because You are my life.

(Continued next page)

When I look down in gloom and despair
I need to look up and know You are there.
When all seems hopeless, You are my hope,
Through Your grace, with my trials I can cope.
Help me to see the little ways
You show Your love
To hear the voice of the Heavenly Dove.
When my life seems barren and dry,
You hear my cry-
You send streams of living water from above.

You are the spring of my life, Lord,
You are the spring of my life.
You are the springs of water,
That never shall run dry.
You are the spring of my life, Lord,
Springs of healing water flowed from your side.
You are the spring of my life
And I shall never thirst again.

Walking along the Creek

It was a beautiful, quiet morning with a temperature of 62 degrees. I enjoyed a slight breeze on my face as I walked along the valley road. A creek winds back and forth through the valley. Several bridges cross over the creek.

I came to the first bridge. I stood looking intently at the quiet flowing water. The beams of sunlight made multiple sparkles upon the water. I walked a little farther and came to the second bridge. At this point the water was flowing more rapidly around large rocks. It gave me a feeling of hurriedness.

At the bottom of the hill is another bridge. Here are two different scenes. - On one side of the bridge the water was calm. The reflection of the bushes, alongside the creek, shone in the water. From the other side of the bridge, I heard the water bubbling noisily over the rocks.

As I thought about these scenes, I remembered the words; *He leads me beside the still water.* Sometimes we have to step from the still water into rocky places. As we let the Son of God shine upon our lives, the sparkle of His presence will be seen through our lives during peaceful times and through the rocky trials.

Gentle Intruder

My doctor advised me to spend time each day in direct sunlight, to receive the benefit of Vitamin D. Today is a beautiful fall day. I set my lawn chair in the position where beams of sunlight would shine across my shoulders and arms. Suddenly, our fluffy, golden haired cat leaped into the chair before I had a chance to sit down. I succeeded in getting her out of the chair; however, she kept rubbing her head against my legs and putting her paws in my lap. I petted her until she was content. Then she ran off to play in the yard.

What did I learn from this incident? I could view this cat as a disruption to my special time alone, or as one of God's beautiful creatures that wanted some tender loving care. Do I recognize God wants to use the disruptions in my life as opportunities to give loving, tender care to hurting people?

Refreshing

This morning as I stepped outside I felt a refreshing, light breeze. The sun was peeping through the trees; the birds were chirping joyful praises to their Creator. I placed my lawn chair in the direct flow of sunlight to get the full benefit of "Vitamin D". Gentle, our golden haired kitty immediately came over to my chair and began rubbing against my legs, showing her affection.

Then I ventured a little farther. Walking down the old familiar path, through the woods, and out into the open field, I noticed clusters of little pink flowers along the roadside.

The time outside this morning was special because the past week has been very hot and humid. It was like a refreshing shower of rain to my soul; although, there was no actual rain from the clouds.

In Acts 3:19 the Bible talks about a refreshing sent from God. *Repent therefore and be converted, that your sins may be blotted out, so that times of refreshing may come from the presence of the Lord,* There is a refreshing in our spirit when the Holy Spirit comes to fill us with His presence. I pray you will sense God's presence in a special way, today

Four Things

I moved my lawn chair out into the driveway where the direct sunlight was shining. In fact, the rays were so bright that I could not look upward. I noticed how the little pebbles in the driveway glistened in the sunlight. Then I noticed a spider moving swiftly just inches above the pebbles. As I watched it going back and forth, suddenly I saw another spider, a short distance from the first one. The second spider was also moving back and forth swiftly. Then I counted five or six spiders all in perfect co-ordination, swiftly, purposefully spinning a network that would be nearly invisible, yet strong.

Proverbs 30:24, 28 says *There are four things which are little upon the earth, but they are exceedingly wise...The spider skillfully grasps with its hands and it is in kings palaces*. What is the wisdom that God has given to spiders? I think it is unity. They all work together purposefully in perfect co-ordination.

The Unoccupied Chair

This morning I took my place sitting in my usual lawn chair out in the sunlight. I felt the warmth of the sun on my legs and arms, as it shone brightly through the tall, stately trees, casting shadows on the path. The sky was deep blue with not a cloud in sight. Listening quietly, I heard the chirping of the birds happily praising their Creator.

But something was different; another lawn chair just like the one I was sitting in had been placed adjacent to my chair. That chair was unoccupied! The two chairs spoke to me of fellowship. I thought about various people whom I would like to "occupy" that chair-my mother, now gone on to glory, my husband who is helping a neighbor today, my sister who is experiencing physical trials and lives so far away, my children and grandchildren who are so lively they can hardly take time to sit down, my friends who are precious every one.

Then I thought about Jesus. Although, I do not see Him with my physical eyes, I know that He is here. I can feel His gentleness and kindness. I feel in awe that the Holy Son of God desires to occupy that empty chair. Since I have invited Jesus Christ to come into my life, He fills that place in my heart that no one else is able to fill. He has promised never to leave. Perhaps you are lonely today, perhaps there is an empty chair in your home. I invite you to let Jesus fill that "empty chair."

MY JOURNEY TO KNOW
GOD'S PURPOSES THROUGH
LIFE'S EXPERIENCES

God's Love Is Like

Thank You, Father for Your love. Your love is like the warmth of a baby wrapped in a warm blanket, snuggled secure in its mother's arms on a cold winter day.

Your Love is Secure.

Your love is like a child's hand firmly grasping his father's hand as they cross a busy street.

Your Love is Protection.

Your love is like a wedding ring, when you trace your finger around and around it, you can find no beginning or end.

Your love is Eternal.

Yet Your love is indescribable, without measure. Your love is shown, most of all, at the cross. Father, thank You for giving Your Only Begotten Son, Jesus Christ, to be the sacrificed for my sin and for the sin of the whole world

Ephesians 3:17-19 *"That Christ may dwell in your hearts through faith; that you, being rooted and grounded in love, may be able to comprehend with all the saints what is the width and length and depth and height- And to know the love of Christ which passes knowledge; that you may be filled with all the fullness of God.*

Complete

On the cross of Calvary,
Jesus died for you and me.
There He shed His precious blood,
That we might be set free.
There He suffered anguish and pain,
Took upon Him all our shame.
Oh glory to His precious Holy Name.
The Son intercedes,
The way to the Father is now prepared.
It's done. It's done.
The covenant is complete between the Father and the Son.
To those who believe, redemption is sealed;
By His stripes sickness is healed.

Peace

All the adult children, aunts, uncles, cousins, and a great company of friends gathered in the church basement for the special celebration of great-grandmother's 90th birthday celebration. One could hear the "buzzing" of many voices. The smell of food was inviting; the cake was beautifully decorated. Cameras were flashing to make special memories.

But above it all I heard a little cry. It was my precious little eight month old grandson. He certainly didn't understand what was going on and was so tired! I took him in my arms and within minutes he was sleeping soundly upon my shoulder.

There is nothing more peaceful than a baby resting with his eyes closed on his mother's shoulder. It reminds me of the words of a song: *Jesus, I Am Resting, Resting in the Joy of What Thou Art, I am finding out the greatness of thy loving heart.* Just before Jesus was to be taken away to die on the cross, He said to his disciples, *Let not your heart be troubled... .peace I leave with you, my peace I give unto you.* John 14:1, 27 In this world of turmoil, heartache, and trouble you may have peace that comes from Jesus. That peace was purchased for you when Jesus died on the cross, arose from the dead, and ascended into heaven where He sits at the right hand of the Father. He is inviting you to come and enter that place of resting in Him.

The Baby's Voice

I remember sitting in the church sanctuary and hearing the voice of my baby in the nursery. I could discern my baby's cry from the cries of the other babies in the nursery. If there are several babies in a nursery, they may all sound alike to strangers; however, each mother will recognize her own baby's cry because that baby is on her heart. I could be washing dishes, cooking a meal, mopping the floor, or doing some other household task, yet I would quickly recognize my baby's cry.

Do I have an ear to hear the voice of my Heavenly Father? Are my spiritual ears in tune to his voice because he is on my heart? Among all voices that demand my attention, do I recognize his voice? I believe the mother's ears are so sensitive to her baby's cry because of the great love a mother has for her baby. It is the same way with our Heavenly Father. Out of his great love He hears the cry of each one of His children. Do I have a great sensitivity to my Father's voice? Psalm 34:15 says, *The eyes of the Lord are on the righteous and His ears are open unto their cry.*

Similarly, a baby will recognize its mother's voice and may not go to another person whose voice they do not know. Father, You said that your sheep know your voice. I am your child; therefore, I will recognize Your voice, even as my babies recognized my voice. Holy Spirit, search my heart that I may know, without a shadow of a doubt, when my Heavenly Father is speaking to me.

Treasures in Christ Jesus

My walk this morning seemed uneventful, absolutely quiet, with a cloudy sky overhead. I began thinking, "Do You have something to tell me today? Is there something more?" Then I realized Your Word says-You have given me all things that pertain to life and godliness, in You are hidden all the treasures of wisdom and knowledge, and I am complete in You. I think about all that You purchased for me. Lord Jesus, by those stripes on Your back flowed down forgiveness, healing, and peace. You have given me abundance of grace. You have given me everything that I need. My part is to understand and appropriate all that You have already given me. How do I receive all these treasures? II Peter 1:4 says that by Your great and precious promises I am made a partaker of Your divine nature; therefore, I can walk today by childlike faith, holding to Your promises as a child holds to his father's hand.

Precious Things

What is the most precious thing to you? Is it your family, your car, your home, friends, reputation, riches, honor, or fame? Did you know if you had abundance of all these things it would not be enough to pay for the one thing which is more precious than anything else in this life? That which is most precious is the ransom of your soul.

God so loved you that He gave that which was most precious to Him, His only Son, to redeem your soul from sin, death, and hell. The precious blood of Jesus paid the price for your salvation.

Those who trust in their wealth And boast in the multitude of their riches, None of them can by any means redeem his brother, Nor give to God a ransom for him-For the redemption of their souls is costly Psalm 49:6-8 *Knowing that you were not redeemed with corruptible things, like silver and gold…but with the precious blood of Christ, as of a lamb without blemish and without spot.* I Peter 1:18-19

Christian, is the Word of God precious to you? Do you realize that the trials you are going through are for the purpose of strengthening your faith? Strong faith is more precious than gold.

I Peter 1:7 *That the genuineness of your faith, being much more precious than gold that perishes, though it is tested by fire, may be found to praise, honor, and glory at the revelation of Jesus Christ.* Where will you place your values today?

Expectation

The air was crisp and cold this morning - 38 degrees with a slight breeze, and a cloudless sky. It took a little longer to get ready for a walk that included putting on layers of clothes, heavy socks, and heavier shoes. I was reminded of when the children were little; we lived up north and snow banks were high. It took almost half an hour to get them all bundled up to go out to play. Then they would be back in five minutes with rosy cheeks and cold noses, ready to come back in the house. The procedure of getting all the coats, boots, gloves, and scarfs off took nearly as long as getting them ready to go outside. But it was worth it!

I could have stayed in the house this morning because it was too cold and took too much time and effort to get all bundled up; however, it was worth it all to sing, dance, and praise the Lord. I had come outside with the expectancy of enjoying my walk and the Lord did not disappoint me

Press On

Press on though the way seems long,
Press on through the night to the light
In the darkest hour,
And press on in the might of His power.

Zacchaeus pressed though the crowd
And climbed a tree to see Jesus.
A woman pressed through the crowd
To touch the hem of His garment

Four men pressed through the roof
To bring their sick friend to Jesus.
Blind Bartimaeus pressed on
To reach Jesus even when he was rebuked.

Chosen

How special it is to be chosen. I think back to when I was last to be chosen on our grade school softball team. Softball wasn't my favorite or accomplished sport! How did I feel when no one wanted me on their team? rejected? lonely? sad? unloved? unneeded? Perhaps, that is how you feel today.

Now think about another scenario.

One day I opened the letter from my husband and read the words, "I want you to marry me...I want you to be my wife." I was chosen to be his bride, chosen to be loved and cared for. How did I feel? I felt accepted, wanted, loved, joyful, and needed.

The Bible says that we have been chosen by God in Christ Jesus to be adopted as His dear children. Christ didn't choose us because of our great ability or outstanding beauty. He chose us when we were lost in sin and at enmity with Him. He chose us to make something beautiful out of our lives for His glory.

Now the choice is yours. Do you choose Christ today? Do you choose to obey Him? Do you choose to let Him make something beautiful out of your life for His glory?

Step-by-Step

Step by step, mile by mile, faithfully walking day after day on the chosen path, sometimes walking slowly, sometimes stopping to ponder the way, sometimes resting, always keeping on to the destiny of home-That describes my morning walks.

Does that describe the Christian walk?

Does it seem monotonous, always the same? Do we sometimes wonder where we are going? Where is this leading us?

When we first begin walking with the Lord, He doesn't require of us giant steps of faith and obedience, but step-by-step He teaches us more of His way.

I think of how step-by-step our little grand children learned to walk. First, they hesitantly took step-by-step; then they proceeded farther across the room; then we heard their feet go pitter-pat, pitter-pat all across the house; finally they were running everywhere. Year by year they steadily grew taller. Sometimes it appeared as if they grew "taller overnight." Other times we saw little change.

Sometimes we ponder about the way God leads us; yet, we keep following Him in the way He has chosen. Sometimes we are growing faster, running, always keeping the destiny of our heavenly home in view. Day by day and with each passing moment, I find strength to walk in His way. Day after day He is changing me. May the likeness of Jesus be seen in me.

Hands... What Meaning They Have!

Etched in my memory is the way my baby's fingers grasped tightly around my little finger giving me a sense of belonging.

When my toddler reached out his hand to hold in mine while we crossed a busy street it gave him a sense of trust.

When my kindergarten child waved good-bye as she stepped into the school bus I felt a sense of letting her go.

When the first little signs of a plant broke through the ground, from the seeds that my children planted with their own hands, they were given a sense of the awesomeness of God's creation.

When my son would not lift his hand to remove the cover from the cookie jar without first asking me; he displayed a sense of honesty.

When my son threw the football that crashed through the kitchen window where I was washing dishes, I experienced a sense of forgiveness.

When my oldest daughter's hands took hold of the steering wheel of our Toyota, for the first time, she was given a sense of responsibility.

When hand written letters came in the mail from daughters who were at college far away, each of us had a sense of loneliness.

(Continued next page)

When I watched the wedding rings being tenderly slipped unto her and his fingers, I had a sense of giving them to one another.

Now, I think about the hands of my Creator,
From Whom all these blessings flow.
I think of the hands of my Savior
Who beckoned for men
To leave their fishing nets and follow Him;

Whose hands held the little child,
Whose hands touched the leper
Making him clean.
Who spoke to the man with the withered hand
And his hand was made whole.

Who took the little maid by the hand,
And she was alive from the dead.
Who laid his hands on the woman who was bent over,
And she was made straight.
Who stretched out his hands on the cross,
That we might have eternal life.

Perfectionism or Love?

In the alcove by my dining room table, hanging over three windows are two green-and-white-checkered curtains. They are made of upholstery fabric which keeps out the heat of the sun in the summer and the cold wind in the winter. When the curtains are open, they are held back with three inch wide strips of white eyelet trim tied into bows. I always tried to tie the bows exactly alike.

One day a dear family member helped me pull the curtains back and tied the bows. Then she went in the other room. I quickly walked over to the windows, untied the bows, and tied them in my fashion. Then I noticed a sad face and understood that someone special wanted to help me. I had not really accepted that loving gesture, but had hurt her by insisting on my own way.

The verse comes to my mind. *He has shown you, what is good; And what does the LORD require of you But to do justly, To love mercy, And to walk humbly with your God* Micah 6:8 The Scripture teaches that we should do everything as unto the Lord. He wants us to do our tasks to the best of our ability. When we put perfectionism ahead of mercy and loving-kindness we become like the Pharisees who lived by the letter of the law.

I Want to Go with You

I bundled up in my blue, warm, fleece jacket, secured my blue and white wool scarf under my chin, and surprised my husband by saying, "I want to go with you. "With a big smile he said, "I will bring the golf cart up by the carport."

I felt like an "old fashioned lady" seated beside my husband on the electric golf cart that belongs to our son. The cart ran so quietly; we could "drink in"the fresh air as we drove through the wooded driveway, and down across the field where the wind was blowing.

As we drove along the gravel road, the invigorating wind blew more directly in our faces. We dropped our letters in the mailbox and turned to go home. We sat quietly enjoying each other's presence.

When we arrived home, my husband said, "It made me so happy to hear you say that you wanted to come with me."Just as my husband delights for me to be in His presence, our Lord Jesus wants us to spend time alone with Him. It delights His heart when we spend time in His presence.

The Light Blue Wool Scarf

Walking briskly the mile to church
Shivering in the cold winter breeze
Blowing across my neck and ears
Then came the gift, the light blue wool scarf
That kept me warm, through the time of storm.

For many years this scarf was kept
With thoughts of one dear friend.
It all began one summer day
When at Bible camp we met.
Although time together was so short
Our letters soon a friendship brought.

An invitation to the city
Was an awesome opportunity
To attend a Christian Keswick Conference,
A tour to the college she loved,
And to visit a great museum.

Two years later at that same school
One day a student was feeling lonely
Ten cents was all the money it took
To make a telephone call.
We met at the bus stop
The weekend was spent at her apartment
Which became for the next three years
"Home away from home"

(Continued next page)

When at my wedding I bid her farewell
I knew our friendship would remain.
To our children she became "Auntie."
I remember the trips we took to visit
And the year we lived in Chicago.
A telephone was needed
To keep safe in the city,
And especially to hear
A voice say, "This is Auntie:"

Then one day we moved
To a state far away;
She was so faithful to keep in touch
Though we were miles apart.
Her letters meant so much.
The years sped by, and then one day
I stopped and knocked upon her door.

Would she remember me?
As we shared memories of long ago
A smile came across her face.
I know we shall meet in heaven one day.
Thank God for His matchless grace.

(In memory of my dear friend, Rachel)

When Nothing Is Left

The last few weeks we have had some beautiful sunny days with temperature in the 70's. I was thinking," Probably we will not need to use our wood stove any longer this spring." This morning was a bit cooler so my son faithfully started a fire in the woodstove.

About noon, I glanced out the kitchen window and noticed a small pile of little branches lying in a scattered pile. I realized these were the same kind of branches that we used in the woodstove.

The thought came to me, "Are these all we have left for the stove?" Then I pictured in my mind a story in the Bible. In this story God sent the prophet Elijah, during the time of famine, to a widow woman to provide food for him. He found the woman gathering a few sticks. She was preparing to bake some bread for herself and her son. She had only a handful of flour and a little oil; when this was gone, she told the prophet, she and her son would eat and die. At Elijah's word, the woman prepared him food first, and according to the Word that God had given Elijah, the bin of flour and the jar of oil did not run out until the time of rain.

I am reminded of another story. When Jesus was in the temple he saw a widow woman put her last mite into the offering. This consisted of her entire living. Do we not serve the same God? In times of uncertainty do we have faith to give, first to the Lord, and believe that He will provide for us, even as He did for the widow?

God's Schedule…. Not Mine

Today is Saturday; I hoped to finish sewing a jumper for my granddaughter whose birthday is today. I will not see her until the end of the month; I will be able to finish sewing by then. She is patiently waiting for me to come and give her the gift. Frequently, I set schedules and deadlines for myself. They have a certain profit; however, I must remember God's plans and time schedule are far more important than mine, and His way is perfect.

You cannot put God in a box to fit your schedule! You cannot say, "I will do this and this," except it is by His will. *Instead you ought to say, If the Lord wills, we shall live and do this or that.* James 4:15. You cannot say, "I will come and repent at a certain time," except it be by His grace. *For the grace of God that brings salvation has appeared to all men.* Titus 2:11 Yet He draws us by His Spirit. So pay attention! Be alert!

Nevertheless, the Scripture says, *And you will seek Me and find Me, when you search for Me with all your heart.* Jeremiah 29:13 Is this a paradox? God cannot lie, neither can He contradict Himself. We cannot understand God's mind and His workings except He reveals Himself by His Spirit. Jesus Christ is the complete revelation of the Father. How easily we go astray from His ways. How mercifully He receives us back, when we turn our hearts again to Him. Let us take time to listen to His voice.

God Is Not in a Hurry

I looked out the window and noticed the sun was shining brightly on my lawn chair. I thought, "I wonder whether I have time to sit outside this morning." Then I thought, "Jesus is there waiting to have fellowship with me." While I sat soaking up the warmth of the sunshine, it took a while to get all the busy thoughts out of my mind. I glanced over at the Allis Chalmers tractor that my husband has for sale. We advertised it in our local classified paper and over the Internet; but we have had little response. We were hoping to use the money for a trip up North, to attend our nephew and niece's wedding anniversary.

My God Is Not in a Hurry

We hurry here and we hurry there
We do not wait for God
To answer our prayer.
We hurry on, over the pathway we run.
We do not wait for God's dear Son.
The Spirit says, "Go" and we say "No,"
Then we miss the Spirit's flow.
We must learn to stop and listen
To know that God is not in a hurry.
He will certainly never worry.
He is never too late and never too early.
He is the one we can trust most surely.

Waiting

Waiting for school to start
Waiting for the school bus
Waiting for college, waiting for graduation
Waiting for the stoplight to change
Waiting for the washing machine to finish the load
Waiting for the elevator to reach the next floor
Waiting to be married
Waiting to be parents
Waiting for dinner to finish cooking
Waiting for the baby to go to sleep
Waiting for the job to be finished
Waiting for the garden to grow
Waiting for that special guest
Waiting for that special vacation
Waiting for the fish to bite the bait
Waiting to be grandparents
Waiting to go home

We spend most of our life waiting. Waiting can be difficult, challenging, and even joyful. All of the waiting mentioned above is temporary. There is a waiting that is eternal that is really worth waiting for...

Looking for the blessed hope and glorious appearing of our great God and Savior Jesus Christ. Titus 2:13

He Is Watching

Today I was baking two big batches of cookies for the campground meetings. I asked my Heavenly Father to help me. He helped me to remember to take each pan out of the oven in time; no cookies were burned. He also showed me I needed to remember He sees everything I do. I ate more cookies than I should have eaten. That might seem insignificant. May my constant thought, in all I do and say, be "What does my Heavenly Father think about this?"

Oh God, You are my God.
You are watching me all the time.
You see me when I stumble.
You see me when I fall.
You hear me when upon your name I call.
You pick me up and set my feet aright.
Oh help me know just what it means
That I am always in Your sight.

Today

Today is a day of Thanksgiving
Today is a day of praise
Today is a day of joyfulness
Today is a day of hope
Today I will sing unto the Lord.

Today, Jesus, I want to walk with You
I want You to be my song all day long
I want to praise You with my whole heart
Thank You that You never will depart.
In everything I do and say
I want on You to rely.
In sweet fellowship
I'll walk and talk with You
And You will show me what to do.

Today may I speak
Words of life, not of death.
Words of faith, not of doubt
Words of hope, not despair
Words of truth, not deceit
Words of love, not of hate
Words that heal, not destroy
Words of light, not of darkness
Words of humility, not of pride.

Today Is a New Page

Today is a new page in the book of my life. This day will be full of choices, opportunities, and decisions. This day will never be available for me to live again.

I have the opportunity to begin the day with praise to my Lord.

I have the opportunity to forgive anyone who would hurt me.

I have the opportunity to trust my Heavenly Father in whatever circumstances this day should bring.

I have the opportunity to grow in grace and in knowledge of my Lord Jesus Christ.

I have the opportunity to be thankful in all things.

I have the opportunity to pray and to read God's Word.

So many of my brothers and sisters do not have freedom to pray or read God's Word without being persecuted. They are blessed to have the opportunity to suffer for Christ's sake.

I have the opportunity to use this day wisely.

Dear Heavenly Father

Dear Heavenly Father,
I give myself to You today.
I present my mind unto You,
My reason, my imaginations, my memory,
That I might have the mind of Christ.

I present my eyes unto You,
That I might see myself as You see me
That I might see others through Your eyes.

I present my ears unto You,
That I might hear Your voice.
I present my mouth unto You,
That I might speak words You give me to speak,
Words of kindness, of truth, and of encouragement.

I present my heart unto You,
That I might love You more and more.
I present my hopes and desires unto You,
That I might fulfill Your desires.

I present my will unto You,
That I might be obedient to You.

I present my hands unto You,
That I might serve others.

I present my feet unto You,
That I might go forth into the places You send me
To share the gospel with those who have never heard.

Accomplishment

Yesterday I finished one of the small goals that I had written on my "to do" list. I put all up- to- date pictures on my baby picture board. They are not babies any longer. All my sweet little grandchildren are growing up. Finishing this task gave me a sense of accomplishment. I nearly finished another small task, putting pictures of my grandchildren on the calendar that I received for Christmas.

Accomplishment is a God given incentive. I read something so special this morning in John chapter 19. It says, *Jesus knowing that all things were finished, gave up His life.* Jesus had the power to lay down His life and to take up His life again. If He had come down from the cross before all was finished, according to God's Word, our salvation would not have been accomplished.

Lord, help me to remember that You, who went all the way to the finish line, are able to give me strength to finish all those tasks, great or small, that You give me to do.

The Finished Task

The seamstress laid each pattern piece on the fabric, meticulously cut the pieces to fit; then spent hours sewing according to the directions. Every possible minute was taken up with this project . Each hand stitch was done with loving care; buttons and lace made the finishing touches. At the end of several days the seamstress sat down in her comfortable chair. She looked with satisfaction at the finished garment...it was a beautiful dress for her granddaughter. Now she could rest. The project was finished.

The carpenter spent many hours shopping for the wood that would best qualify for the project. He carefully followed the plans that were laid out. Every measurement must be accurate, every piece must be in proper alignment; it must be strong enough to stand amidst strong winds, tight enough to prevent any moisture from entering.

Days, weeks, months, and even years went by. The vision that the carpenter had never diminished. In the woods one could hear the pounding of the hammer and the buzz of the saw; until one day all was silent. The carpenter opened the door for his wife to enter the beautiful home that he had built with his own hands. Now he could rest because all was finished.

The author was continually- looking for illustrations, noticing picturesque scenes, colorful sunsets, thinking about what the Creator was saying. Quiet listening is required to express such pictures into words.

Then there was preparation in organizing the material that would effectively tell the reader what is on the heart of the writer. After all is ready the manuscript must go to the printer or publisher to be searched over and over again for any flaws or corrections. Finally, the illustrations put on paper become reality in the form of a finished book. The author rejoices that his work is now complete.

Our lives are like a book, page after page being written as we live moment by moment. God is the author who is able to take what is in our hearts and turn it into a beautiful picture for His glory.

What satisfaction is found when a project is finished! Whether one is -an artist, a cook, a carpenter, a seamstress, an author, or anyone with a purpose and a project to be finished, it is with a sense of joy that one can at last rest from their labor, knowing the work has been completed.

While this is true in the natural realm, how much more it is true in the spiritual realm. Hebrews 1:3 says, *Who being the brightness of His glory and the express image of His person, and upholding all things by* the *word of his power, when He had by Himself purged our sins, sat down at the right hand of the Majesty on high.* Jesus sat down on the right hand of the Father after he finished the work that he came to do.

(Continued next page)

That work was gloriously finished after He bore all of our sins and sicknesses on the cross and rose up triumphantly from the grave.

Jesus carried out every single act of healing, of preaching, of selecting and training his disciples that the Father had sent Him to do before the cross as well as fulfilling the ultimate purpose of God in laying down His life for everyone who would believe in Him.

We have tasks to do while we live here on this earth, and it is satisfying to finish those tasks. Ephesians 2:10 says, *For we are His workmanship, created in Christ Jesus for good works, which God prepared beforehand that we should walk in them.*

It is awesome that the God who created us has plans for each one of us to carry out. We may not have finished that work before Jesus comes or before we are taken out of this life, but may our goal be as Paul's goal was when he said in 2 Timothy 4:7, *I have fought the good fight, I have finished the course, I have kept the faith.*

Extended Time

Dinner is ready to be served-rice and meatloaf have been reheated in the microwave and held on keep warm setting, the table has been set, crisp salad with Western Dressing is ready in the refrigerator; fresh tap water fills the glasses. But first the mail must be opened and the cats fed. A little extended time is needed.

I have been waiting eagerly for the first book that I published to come in the mail. It was shipped overnight on January 31st. Today is February 7th. I just found out that my book is in Dallas and should be here tomorrow. I can hardly wait! Time was extended due to massive snowstorms throughout many areas of the country.

These extended times are simply "everyday living." There are more serious extended times such as- having loved ones in the hospital waiting, hoping to see what the outcome will be, airports closed due to storms, highways closed, unable to get home.

What do I do with extended times? Do I see that time as an opportunity to reach out to others, as an opportunity to be patient, kind, thankful, even joyful, knowing that God has everything in control. Do I see it as an opportunity to cast all my care upon the One who loves me so? What does God think of extended time? He is in charge and is able to extend time whenever He sees fit.

For Joshua, he caused the sun to be still for one whole day; for Hezekiah, he granted fifteen years to live. Someday there will be no more extended time to repent, no more time to get right with God, no more time to live for Jesus.

A Time to Leave

On the wall by my computer is a beautiful picture of my four precious grandchildren. They are walking hand in hand across the driveway on our field. My husband says they are stepping out into life. Many times we have to leave the comfort zones of our lives and go forward step by step to follow Jesus. As I think about this I am reminded of...

My first time away from home without knowing anyone else at a Bible camp 250 miles from home (this decision made a lasting effect on my life)

Leaving my twin sister to go to a different college than she would be attending...

Standing at the altar on my wedding day, making the commitment to leave my mom and dad, to cleave to my husband...

Watching our children step upon the school bus their first day of kindergarten...Tears shed months before they graduated from high school, knowing they would be leaving home...

Leaving our home in Wisconsin to move to Texas (1000 miles from our friends and relatives)...

Stepping into an airplane, going across the ocean (leaving behind all familiar culture) to carry the precious Word of Life...

These times mean so much to us. They bring back so many precious memories; yet there is another leaving that transcends all others.

Someday Soon

Someday soon we will be leaving this life
And all the sweet memories
Will dull at the sight,
At the splendor of Heaven with glory so bright.
When we see the Face
Of our Savior so dear,
From grief of the past
He will wipe every tear.
Trials will be finished at last.

A Window of Time

Dark clouds were slowly moving, with just a small "window" of blue sky peeking through a tiny silver lining on a small cloud. Before long that window closed. God is giving us a window of time to repent before He sends the storms. There is a window of grace before He returns; and that window will be closed forever.

The clouds were hanging in space; athough they looked like they would be full of rain, no raindrops were coming. God made the clouds. God made the wind. God is in control. But God gave me the choice whether to let Him be in control of my life, or to attempt to control my own life.

Peace in the Time of Storm

You have taken all my sins away.
You are the Truth, the Life, and the Way.
When the devil comes with his doubts and lies
I will flee to your nail pierced side
There is proof that in your love I abide.
Lord, grant in the storms of life
Above the noise of clamor and strife
I may hear your voice
Giving me quiet assurance.
When I would falter, grasp my hand.
I know that You will never let me go.
You pick me up from sinking sand
And place me firm on heaven's land.

Jean Mattson ℘

Which Cup?

Running over, running over, my cup is full and running over; Since the Lord saved me, I'm as happy as can be. My cup is full and running over. I sang these words as I was sitting in the lawn chair in my friend's back yard. I sang this chorus to my friend's little daughter. It was a chorus that I used to teach children many years ago. It is a fun chorus for children with actions to go with the words.

I began to think about the words. What do they really mean? Psalm 116:13 says, *I will take up the cup of salvation and call upon the name of the Lord.* Jesus, when praying in the garden of Gethsemane, said, *"Oh my Father, if it be possible let this cup pass from me,"* Jesus took upon Himself the wrath of God which we deserved for our sins. The cup of salvation is to receive the gift of eternal salvation that Jesus purchased for us when He died upon the cross for our sins.

Along with the cup of salvation are countless blessings such as- healing, provision, protection, wisdom, and all the spiritual blessings in Christ Jesus. When the Lord saves us we can be, "happy as can be," because our "cups" are running over with the blessings God has to offer us.

The Bible also talks about the cup of God's wrath. Jesus drank of the cup of God's wrath for all mankind when He died upon the cross. *He who believes in the Son has everlasting life and he who does not believe in the Son shall not see life, but the wrath of God abides on him.* John 3:36. It is my prayer that whoever reads this writing will receive the cup of God's salvation, not of God's wrath.

MY JOURNEY TO KNOW GOD'S WAYS THROUGH OTHER CULTURES

Turn Aside

Turn aside, just do not walk away.
Turn aside and open your eyes.
Turn aside and listen
To their voices.

Just as Moses turned aside
To see the burning bush;
Turn aside from your busy life
To see what God would say.

My people are in bondage
They sit in prison cells
Your prayers can bring deliverance
And grace to face each day.

Homeless, weary, and hungry,
Lonely, helpless, and sad,
They are partakers of Christ's suffering.
Let them know that you care
By your letter, with them share.

Unfinished Tasks, Disrupted Lives

I hurriedly walked toward the door to sit outside in the sunlight. I noticed the breakfast table needed clearing. I quickly put away food that needed refrigeration and rinsed out the soiled dishes to be put into the dishwasher. I went in to the bedroom; on the desk was the check that was half written out. I had intended to send it with my husband to put in the mail today.

Unfinished tasks, interrupted lives, as I think about these little insignificant things in life, my mind turns to my brothers and sisters in many countries of the world. They may be going through very significant disruptions. Because of their faith in Christ, they may be taken from their homes at any time, kidnapped, or hauled off to jail. There may be no time to change their clothes or finish their meal. Today, their plans may be to teach a Bible class or to work in the fields, while their husbands go on an evangelistic tour. Today, these plans may be greatly changed. Today, their lives may be suddenly ended.

Lord, may I not be annoyed or discouraged by interruptions or unfinished tasks in my daily life; instead may they be reminders for me to pray for my "persecuted family," whose lives will be greatly disrupted and changed this day.

Darkness Cannot Prevail

This morning it was light outside but I did not see the sun shining as I walked down the driveway. I wondered, "Why do I not see the brightness of the sun?" Then suddenly, I saw a faint sign of sunrays just above the thickness of the green trees. Then a very tiny red light was seen in the center of the green trees. Several minutes later I could see the shape of the entire sun, red in color.

I thought, "It is this way with the Lord." Sometimes I do not see His presence.; nevertheless, the darkness cannot comprehend the light. The darkness of this world cannot overcome the light of Jesus. Though there be a very faint light; though it seems like Christianity would be wiped out; yet, the darkness cannot entirely extinguish that Light of Jesus.

In the country of North Korea there is almost total spiritual darkness. Many North Koreans who escape into China become Christians when they hear the gospel message. Then they choose to go back to North Korea and share the gospel, knowing they face imprisonment in a labor camp or death if their Christian witness is discovered. Pray for them that they may have strength and grace to overcome as they face great persecution. John 1:5 says,. *And the light shines in the darkness and the darkness did not comprehend it. .* Jesus is that Light of Life who cannot be extinguished in North Korea.

Treasures of Darkness

Isaiah 45:3 says, *I will give you the treasures of darkness and hidden riches of secret places.*

Lord, just to know your presence intimately, walking moment by moment is my goal. That secret place isn't necessarily a physical area, but a place of communion with You, where all other voices are shut out.

My brothers and sisters in refugee camps and prisons are able to experience that secret place. My heart is stirred, as I look at the pictures of the orphan children in Burma. With eyes closed and hands raised in worship, their faces are filled with the sweet presence of the Lord.

What are the treasures of darkness? II Corinthians 4:6 says, *For it is God who commanded light to shine out of darkness who has shone in our hearts to give the light of the knowledge of the glory of God in the face of Jesus Christ.*

I believe the glory of God's presence is the treasure of darkness. Stephen saw that glory; outwardly his face was transformed. In my darkest hour God is able to open my eyes to see the glory of God.

God Sees

This morning I kept noticing, in the pathway, little insects that had died and were being eaten up by ants. It was a rather repulsive thing to see. It was a picture of death and destruction. I shudder to think about the death and destruction that is going on in the world today.

God sees the heartaches, grief, pain, and suffering that are going on in this world; He sees the destruction and terror. Psalm 102:19-20 tells us that *He looked down from the height of His sanctuary: From heaven the LORD viewed the earth, To hear the groaning of the prisoner, To release those appointed to death.* In Psalm 84 when talking about those who pass through, "a place of weeping," verse seven says, *they go from strength to strength, Each one appears before God in Zion.*

So what should my response be to the suffering that is going on in the world? I am reminded about the parable that Jesus told when He was asked, "Who is my neighbor?" *Then Jesus answered and said, A certain man went down from Jerusalem to Jericho and fell among thieves, who stripped him of his clothing, wounded him, and departed, leaving him half dead.* Luke10:39

Then Jesus told of the response of the priest, the Levite, and the Samaritan. Verse 33-34: *But a certain Samaritan, as he journeyed, came where he was. And when he saw him he had compassion . So he went to him and bandaged his wounds, pouring on oil and wine; and he set him on his own animal, brought him to an inn, and took care of him.*

In the back of my book I have included information that you may find helpful in responding to the suffering that is going on in the world today.

God Is Good

This morning was a chilly 40 degrees; however, there was very little breeze and I felt the warmth of the sun on my back. The dew is on the hayfield where little flowers are beginning to show their appearance. I thought about the goodness of the Lord. The words of a little chorus came to my mind, *Oh God is good, Oh God is good, and Oh God is good, He's so good to me...* David, in the Psalm 27:13 said, *I would have lost heart, unless I had believed that I would see the goodness of the Lord in the land of the living.* Psalm 145:9 says, *The Lord is good to all, And His tender mercies are over all His works.*

Even in prison camp Corrie ten Boom was able to discern the goodness of the Lord in dire circumstances. Psalm 107 brought strength and courage to Sabina Wurmbrand when she was in prison for her witness for Christ. Psalm 107:8 says, *Oh that men would give thanks to the LORD for His goodness, And for His wonderful works to the children of men.*

Lord, let my focus be on your goodness, for You are a good God, not evil. Goodness is part of Your character.

His Eyes Are upon You

I looked up and noticed the moon in the clear sky. It looked like it was hanging there in space with nothing holding it; but I know that my Lord is holding the moon in space even as He is holding the earth and all creation in His hands. That is awesome! The same Lord has His eyes on me.

When I first began walking I was singing, "My eyes are on You, Lord, my eyes are on You, "and then my eyes wandered to a pickup that was setting on the road across the field. I began thinking, "What if that is someone who is waiting to come after me?" Then I thought about my brother and sisters in Christ who are literally being chased by the enemy, having their homes burned, chased into the jungles, or refugee camps. I began to pray for them.

Oh Lord Jesus, You entered into humanity that You might experience every single trial and suffering of mankind, that you might experience grief, heartache and sorrow. You became one of us, except without sin, and You are calling those who are yours to follow You, to the point of losing ourselves from our own petty desires, to identify with the fears, sorrows, and burdens of our brothers and sisters who are suffering for You.

I am able to do this by prayer, by seeking Your face, and by seeing them through Your eyes. Lord Jesus, through the power of the Holy Spirit in my life, please break through any callousness, coldness, and indifference in my heart. Let me be touched by the sufferings of my brothers and sisters.

Remembering Our
<u>Persecuted Family</u>

This morning Rupert and I walked a little later, the sun had already begun to rise in the sky. The temperature was a cool 60 degrees with a slight breeze. There was just a bit of dew left on the grass. When we were near the main road, I saw something which looked like a snake or a rope sprawled out on the road. I didn't go any farther. If Rupert tangled with a snake he wouldn't know what to do. We ran for a little ways.

I began to think about my brothers and sisters in Christ who have to flee from their homes. The forest and mountain dens are the only place to go. I prayed for them-that You, Lord, would give them strength when they are weary, that they might find safe places that You would give them grace to go through their trials. I began to think of Scriptures say that You are our hiding place. I prayed that my brothers and sisters will sense your presence in a very real way. Psalm 32:7 says, *You are my hiding place; You shall preserve me from trouble; You shall surround me with songs of deliverance.*

Marching

This morning the driveway was muddy. I wore my plastic rubbers over my shoes. I walked on the road that goes through the field. I could hear the "scrape, scrape" of my rubbers on the little rocks in the road. It reminded me of the sound of marching.

I prayed for soldiers who are marching. Lord, strengthen them, deliver them from the enemy, comfort them, give them wisdom, and help them to know Your presence. I prayed for my brothers and sisters who are marching to work all day in labor camps where they are being persecuted for their witness for You, Lord. May they also know Your strength. You have promised that You will not allow us to be tempted above our strength, but You will provide a way of escape that we may be able to bear it. I prayed for those who are marching to refugee camps. I cannot imagine what it must be like for them, but I hold them up before You, Lord. May they know that You are their refuge and salvation. Miraculously provide for their physical and emotional needs.

My Eyes Are on You, Lord

My eyes are on You, Lord,
My eyes are on You
And when my gaze would wander
Into the camp of the enemy
Or look too intently
At that which is temporary-

Then bring me back
Lord, to know –
That Your eyes are on me
From Your presence
I cannot flee
Because Your eyes
Lord, are upon me.

Your eyes are on me, Lord
Your eyes are upon me
And when the storm clouds gather
And I cannot clearly see Your face
Then Lord, let me remember
Your everlasting grace.

Come Along With Me on a Trip to China

For weeks I prepared to go on this mission trip. I was blessed when our pastor and church congregation prayed for me. We were on our way to Ft Worth to stay overnight with our son's mother and father -in-law. There was only one thing lacking! Karen, my team leader called to ask for prayer. Her exact words were "If the Lord doesn't meet my financial need by tomorrow night I will not be going." I tried to reach Karen by phone but no answer. I believed that the Lord would have me go on this trip to China so I continued to go to Ft. Worth.

At 12AM I awoke and three Scriptures came to my mind. *Therefore do not cast not away your confidence, which has great* reward. Hebrews 10:35...*Trust in the Lord with all your heart and lean not unto your own understanding; In all your ways acknowledge Him, and He shall direct your paths.* Proverbs 3:4-5. *You will keep him in perfect peace, Whose mind is stayed on You, Because he trusts in You..* Isaiah 26:3

I was able to get a few more hours of restful sleep. I called Karen and my heart was filled with joy as I heard her say, "The Lord supplied yesterday, I am going". My husband drove me to the airport and went with me to the gate. I boarded the plane for San Francisco. Arriving there I wondered, "How will I find Karen?" We did not have pictures of each other, nor did we know what color clothing each other was wearing. I reached the departure gate where we were supposed to meet; than turned around to start back the way I had come. (Continued next page)

Suddenly I knew, as I looked into the eyes of a tall, pleasant woman walking toward me, that this was Karen. As our eyes made contact, she immediately recognized me. She knew Julia, another team member.

The third team member, John, was much younger than us three women, but very capable. He met us at the gate. I will always remember the thrill of meeting Karen face to face at the airport. Someday we will meet Jesus Christ face to face. I am reminded of the Scripture which says, *we shall see Him as He is* I John 3:2. We shall also recognize Him by the nail prints in His hands. Before you meet Jesus face to face you need to meet Him as your Savior and Lord.

Have You Met Jesus

Have you met Jesus, as you walk along life's way?
Have you experienced His touch upon your soul?
Do you know that He can make you whole?
He can wash away your sin;
Make you pure and whole within.
Have you met Jesus? Have you seen His face?
Do you know that it is filled with mercy and grace?
When you come to Him in faith,
He'll not turn you away.
Come to Him today.

By Love Serve One Another

Our little group became very close knit. Each one of us has different backgrounds; but, we all had one purpose, to serve our brothers and sisters who are being persecuted for their faith. We arrived in China at 5pm. We were amazed as we walked through the airport; no inspection tables were to be seen, no policeman in sight. We walked right out to the taxi area and piled into a van for the drive to the motel. The motel was an hour away from the airport. Karen, John, and Julia all were so kind to help me with the heavy suitcases. While staying at the motel, Karen invited us to come to her room that we might have devotions together.

I realize now, in a new way, that my being perfected in Christ is part of the perfection of the whole body of Christ. Each member of the body of Christ is so important to the growth and development of the entire body; just as each part of our physical body is so important to our whole being. When one member suffers, the other members suffer with it. The Lord wants us to learn to "suffer" with our brothers and sisters who are persecuted for their faith by coming along side with them in prayer and other ways that He gives us opportunity. Ephesians 4:13 says, *Til we all come to the unity of the faith and of the knowledge of the Son of God, to a perfect man, to the measure of the stature of the fullness of Christ.*

Culture Shock

Learning to eat with chopsticks, drinking from tiny teacups, dodging buses, cars, motorcycles, all in attempts to cross the street, purchasing a pair of winter boots from a saleslady who only spoke Chinese, hurrying through throngs of people to reach the train before it left the station-all of these experiences were exciting, invigorating, sometimes scary; but, I did not consider them as culture shock.

It was just past midnight when we boarded the train. The sleeper cars were equipped with compartments which held six bunk beds, three on each side, with a little table by the window at one end. In our compartment John and Karen took the middle bunks; Julia and I had the bottom bunks. We were all very tired and I fell asleep before the others.

About 2:30 am I woke up and saw someone looking under the bunk. Our luggage was stored under the bottom bunk. I saw a strange man and thought he was trying to steal my shoe. I grabbed my shoe and hollered, "What are you doing?...don't take my shoe." Karen awoke and explained to me that a Chinese man was sleeping on the top bunk. He was looking for his own shoes. She talked to him in Chinese and he seemed to be understanding.

I was very embarrassed to think that I had hollered in English at a poor Chinese man who didn't understand a word that I said. That was a true symptom of culture shock, also a true lesson in humility.

Beautiful Canaan Hymns

7AM Upon awakening I heard music playing over the train's loud speaker. It sounded like the music of the Canaan Hymns which I had I spent many hours listening to on a DVD weeks before I came to China. The words on the DVD were translated into English. The hymns were written by a Chinese Christian peasant girl. Now, as I listened to the instrumental music I wondered, "Could this really be these same Canaan hymns?" I thought, "Lord, You have brought me to the country where my brothers and sisters are being persecuted for Your sake." I looked out the window; the countryside reminded me of the peasant song writer. Tears ran down my cheeks, as I remembered the testimony of her life.

8AM There was opportunity to buy various kinds of food. We chose Chinese noodles, rice and tea? Does that sound like a good enough Chinese breakfast? I began to understand why Becca, my little Chinese granddaughter, likes noodles so well. We each had our own thermos of tea. Chopsticks were provided. Later on that day we bought some of the largest, sweetest, purple grapes that I have ever seen. I was reminded that Jesus drank of the fruit of the vine with his disciples. The fruit of the vine represents the blood of Jesus that cleanses our hearts from sin.

There was time for each member or our team to talk about our experiences on this trip. We felt a close bond with one another. Living together in the same little compartment for 36 hours could be grace testing; however, I don't remember even one cross word spoken among us.

Silent Night

We flew nearly all day from Hong Kong to Northwest China. Arriving at our destination, we found snow falling and near zero degrees weather. It reminded me of the coldness of the border guards and of Communism in general. We arrived at the Holiday Inn. How surprised I was to see Christmas decorations all over the hotel. After transporting our luggage to our rooms we all came to the spacious dining room for a late dinner. The buffet offered a large selection of Chinese food along with some American dishes. I sat down to enjoy my meal. Suddenly I heard violin music playing "Silent Night." Tears came to my eyes.

Even though the Christmas Carols were being played to influence the tourists, I realized that a government cannot silence God. Instead, let the entire world be put to silence. God is on His throne!

Back in our room we gathered for devotions. John was singing, *God is a good God, He is a great God, He can do anything but fail. He has moved so many mountains out of my way. God is a wonderful God.*

In the evening we visited another contact person, and walked to a Muslim restaurant. We were seated around a large rectangle table in a private room. The walls were decorated with beautiful stained glass mirrors. The young waitresses were dressed in their tribal costumes. They did an excellent job serving our meal. I would have liked to hug them and tell them how much Jesus loves them. Of course, they couldn't understand English. Karen helped us understand the menu and interpreted for us. Perhaps, in some way, they could sense the love of Jesus through our lives.

God's Heart for China

I never realized what an immense country China is until I spent two weeks flying and riding the train from place to place. Then I had only scratched the surface so to speak. The Great Wall is insurmountable in construction, beauty. and breath taking to see. I climbed 200 steps, and then stopped counting. I never reached the top.

I was deeply impressed with the throngs of people, especially in the cities. In the railway station one could almost be pushed along with the crowd. I remember the Muslim culture in the North West and the beautiful young waitresses, dressed in their native costumes. These were all parts of China that we were able to see; however, there was a part of China that we were not able to see.

We did not come face to face with our brothers and sisters in Christ who are suffering persecution for their faith. It would have been dangerous for them to be found with believers from the United States. As I left China, I felt as if part of my heart was there. God's heart is also on China. He sent His Son to die for every one of those throngs of people. Pray for boldness, courage, and grace for those in China who are paying a great cost for their faith. Pray for a mighty outpouring of His Spirit in the church in China

Who Are These?

Who are these, can they be counted?
Passing through the valley of Baca
On their way to eternal bliss;
Faces uplifted to the Father
Tear stained
Showing pain
Suffering shame for the Father's name.
Homeless
Lonely
Wounded just as you were, Lord.

I have a warm, cozy bed
With plenty of covers over my head;
They are shivering in prison cells
No pillows for their heads
With only cement floors for their bed.
If I am hungry to my cupboard I go
A supply of food will be there I know;
In the refugee camps they lay
Many are starving every day.

I go to my closet to decide what to wear
Mix or match I have such a choice;
Their clothes are tattered rags
With barely enough to cover their back.

When I suffer bruises or breaks
A trip to the doctor is all that it takes;
They are bruised from tortures sore
With no medicine on their wounds to pour.

When I am lonely many friends I can call
On any occasion;
They sit alone in isolation.
These are my brothers; these are my sisters in Christ.

Circles

This morning Rupert kept running around in circles, running ahead of me, and circling around me all along the path. I began to think about circles. Isaiah 40:22 says, *It is He who sits above the circle of the earth, And its inhabitants are like grasshoppers, Who stretches out the heavens like a curtain, And spreads them out like a tent to dwell in.* This speaks to me that God is over all and much greater than man. Yet, He is concerned about every individual.

I remember reading the testimony of Arthur Matthews, a missionary to China. Mr. Matthews was one of the last missionaries to leave China before the Communists took over in 1949. He stated that there was no safer place than in the center of the circle of God's will. He and his wife strongly felt the Lord's presence around them there in China while they were waiting to get connections to come to the United States.

As I kept walking, I began to feel the warmth of the sun on my back. God even made the sun to run its circuit. Speaking about the sun, Psalm 19:6 says, *Its rising is from one end of the heaven, and its circuit to the other end; and there is nothing hidden from its heat.* My prayer is: Lord, keep me and everyone who is reading this in the center of the circle of Your will.

Contentment

This morning as I walked out into the field and looked up into the sky I saw the longest jet stream that I have ever seen. It seemed to stay in view all during my walk to the gate and back. It reminded me of flying; and I thought about my desire to go to China again or to another foreign land. I began to think about the song that our church choir was singing last Sunday evening. *If Jesus goes with me I'll go anywhere.* I have known the song for many years; however, I never thought much about the words of one stanza of the song which says, *If Jesus goes with me I'll stay anywhere.* It is talking about being willing to stay home, if that is what God is telling me to do.

Paul in Philippians 4:11 says, *I have learned in whatever state I am to be content.* Webster's dictionary's definition of contentment includes-satisfying, to fulfill needs and desires. If I am satisfied with Jesus I can truly be content whether I go on a mission trip or stay home.

Reflection

This morning was a cool, cloudy day with a refreshing wind blowing across the field. The neighbor's cows were kicking up their heels, prancing lively about the field. Rupert was bounding up the path; everything spoke of life. I felt like jumping, dancing, and praising the Lord. I sang, "Blow, blow, wind of the Spirit, and blow across my soul. Blow, blow, wind of the Spirit, blow away all chaff until the reflection of Jesus is clearly seen."

When I was seven years old I used to stand by the riverbank in front of my grandparents' home. When the river was real clear I would throw in a little stone, and watch the ripples go farther and farther away. If the river was not clear I could not see the ripples. If the river was clear I could also see my reflection.

The "River of Life" in me wants to ripple out to others-first Jerusalem (those closest to me), then Judea (those that I rub elbows with every day), and Samaria (those who I may find it harder to relate to), and then to the uttermost parts of the earth, (those very far away).

Lift up Your Voice

Lift up your voice unto the Lord
Who in His holy temple dwells.
Lift up your voice in humility
With hearts of truth and purity.

Lift up your voice unto the King
Lift up your voice in prayer
For those who are oppressed
That they may know their cry is heard.

Lift up your voice in strength.
Be not afraid to stand
For truth and righteousness.

Lift up your voice that all may hear
The gospel message true and clear.
That none may say, "I never knew."
Lift up your voice, proclaim the Word
That Jesus Christ salvation brings
Be not ashamed to make Him known.

"I cried to the Lord with my voice
And He heard me from His holy hill"
Psalm 3:4

What a Privilege

As the plane began descending through the clouds, out of the window I saw the beautiful green countryside. Tears came to my eyes as I thought of the privilege of stepping on the same soil where Christians are being persecuted. This story began after my husband and I had filled out applications to go on various mission trips. One fall day when I had just stepped into the house from work, I answered the phone and heard a voice say," We have room for your husband and you to go on a mission trip in a few weeks." This was the Lord's timing since I had just told my supervisor at work that I would be working on call instead of full time.

Much preparation was needed to get ready to go across the ocean to a land where we would not know the language or the culture; however, our hearts were filled with joy knowing that we would have a part in blessing our brothers and sisters who are persecuted for Christ's sake.

Our journey began in Dallas, TX, where we met our first team member. When we reached Los Angeles we met three other team members. I was especially blessed to see my "big sis" from college days who lives in Los Angeles. We had not seen each other for twenty years, and had a great visit at the airport. It was a nineteen hour flight to our destination. We arrived at Bangkok, Thailand at 10 pm.

We were thankful to get through customs without any delays. We took a taxi to a nearby hotel, and slept a few hours before returning to the airport. This time we boarded a smaller plane. The customs authorities questioned one of our team members. We all prayed and God answered. When we went through customs at Vientiane, Laos, we met our team leader for the first time. She had spent several years leading mission trips and understood the Laotian language and customs. We were instructed to act like tourists. The hotel staff was very courteous. The tables in the dining room were decorated with orchids.

On Sunday morning each one of us made our way to our team leader's room with suitcases full of Bibles. After spending time in prayer, we all walked down to the dining room. After lunch, our team leader and one of the team members quietly left the room while the rest of us stayed in the dining room. We waited, (for what seemed like hours) until our team leader came back to the hotel. We again gathered in her room and rejoiced to hear the Bibles were safe in the hands of our contact person.

Love Is a Universal Language

We took a bus tour to a tribal village. The people are very poor and live in primitive conditions up in the foothills of the mountains. The women do very beautiful handwork, which they sell in the market. They receive very little pay for their hours of labor. We bought several pieces of embroidered cloth, and gave the children candy. Our bus driver took us up in the mountains to Lake Nam Ngum. We ate lunch at the restaurant. The native people are so humble and eager to serve. The main dish was rice; the various dishes to go with it were quite spicy.

After lunch we rode on an open sided wooden boat to another village at the end of the lake. The people lived in thatched roof houses. About thirty or forty children stood curiously, shyly watching us. My husband sat down on the threshold of one of the homes. The children smiled at him. They could tell he loved them as he reached out his hands to them. Love is a universal language. I wondered, "Will some of the people in this village receive one of the Bibles that we have brought to Laos?" Pray for them. The Bible says there will be some from every tribe, and tongue, and nation worshipping Jesus in heaven.

Eyes That Cannot See
Ears That Cannot Hear

On our last day in Laos, we took another boat trip up the Mekong River that separates Laos from Thailand. Thailand is a very strong Buddhist country. By the side of the river on the Thailand side is a large monastery where Buddhist monks are trained; directly opposite on the Laos side is a Buddhist temple. The captain stopped our boat near the shore. We climbed some wide stone steps. We were surprised to see, at a little distance, a huge statue of Buddha. We felt sad as we watched the captain of our boat bow down to this dead idol.

I thought of the words in Psalm 115:4-7 *Their idols are silver and gold, the work of men's hands, They have mouths, but they speak not; eyes have they, but they see not; They have ears, but they hear not; noses have they, but they smell not; They have hands, but they handle not; feet have they, but they walk not; neither speak they through their throat.* We prayed for all people who are bowing to idols that their spiritual eyes would be opened to the glorious gospel of Christ.

Special Anniversary

We flew back to Bangkok and from there to Ho Chi Minh City that has a population of seven million people. The traffic there is indescribable. Numberless motor bikes skillfully made their way around the buses and throngs of people. Open shops lined the streets. Everywhere we looked we saw children begging and people with outstretched hands and pleading eyes.

We went on a tour bus to a city by the South China Sea. We stayed overnight at a hotel where we met some of our Vietnamese brothers and sisters in Christ. They shared their testimonies with us. They were joyful as they told about the miracles God had been doing among their people. They have great boldness to stand for the Lord. Their passion is to bring the gospel to all of the tribes in their country who have never heard the Name of Jesus. They are willing to suffer persecution for the cause of Christ.

The next day we ate lunch at a restaurant by the seaside. The fresh breeze from the sea was invigorating. When we had nearly finished our meal, my husband and I had a real surprise. Someone had ordered a special cake for our 38th wedding anniversary! We felt joy, for the love shown to us by our Vietnamese friends; and we felt sad, knowing that many of our brothers and sisters could easily be separated from their loved ones and put in prison for their testimony for the Lord.

My Brother's Feet

When I was resting on the couch this morning I felt the warmness of the sun shining through the window. It felt especially good on my bare feet. Then I began to think about some other feet.

Feet with no shoes on cold prison floors-
Feet blistered and torn with festering sores-
Feet that are running through jungles and field-
Feet that are weary and hardly can walk.

These are the feet of my brothers and sisters.
Their feet are following the Lamb wherever He goes.
Their feet are shod with the Gospel of peace.
They keep going to the ends of the earth.

I thought about the woman whose
Teardrops fell as she washed Jesus' feet.
As I kneel in prayer for my persecuted family,
May I "wash their feet" with tears of love.

JOURNEY'S END...THE ULTIMATE GOAL

Jesus Will Outshine Them All

Driving home from Hillsboro, my husband and I saw the most beautiful sunset. The entire sky was filled with clouds of various colors and designs. To the west were feathery cloud formations that shone with an orange-golden hue; to the south were pink-reddish clouds that had a rippling look. As we drove on, we noticed a feathery cloud that reminded me of a jet stream. It lay diagonally across the sky for a very long distance, having a pink glow at one end gradually turning to white at the smaller end. As I thought about the beautiful picture that God had painted, my husband began to sing a song about heaven.

Mansions will glisten on the hills of glory,
Happy reunion on streets of gold.
Angel choirs singing glad praises forever,
But Jesus will outshine them all

Just a Foretaste

This morning I was happy to walk at daybreak. It was a glorious 60 degrees that was a contrast to the 80 degree temperature that had encompassed my walks lately. As I entered the open field and looked up into the sky, The Lord painted such a magnificent picture. The blue sky was peeking through clusters of clouds. In the Eastern sky, rays of brightness shone upon tiny clouds giving them a pink and silver lining. It reminded me of a song I used to sing when I was a child:

Back of the clouds, the sun is always shining
After the storms your skies will all be blue.
God has prepared a rosy tinted lining
Back of the clouds its waiting to shine through.

As I thought upon the words of that song, suddenly, I noticed all of the clouds had "pink and silver linings," as the sun was beginning to shine on them. The first beautiful picture in the sky had turned into a greater degree of glory. The first was a foretaste of that to come. I began to sing:

Just a foretaste of Your glory, just a foretaste of Your might
Just a foretaste of Your beauty, and Your glorious power
Just a foretaste of Your love, just a foretaste of Your joy
Just a foretaste of Your peace, just a foretaste Your holiness
Just a foretaste here below.

Homesick for Heaven

No more heartbreak, no more pain,
No more loss, only gain,
No more shame, no more sin
Only pureness within,
No more loneliness, no more fear
God shall wipe away each tear.

No more weariness. No condemnation
No more burdens to bear
Living forever in His loving care,
Looking to see those
Who have gone on before
Blessed reunion
With loved ones so dear.

Brothers and sisters will be there from every nation
What an awesome celebration.
Glory beyond what words can express
Above all else...
Fellowship sweet at Jesus feet
Touching the nail prints in His hands
Seeing the tender love in His eyes
Hearing words of acceptance in His voice
That will be glory for me

Only One Thing

When I stand before God's throne
Only one question of importance will be.
What have you done with my Son?
Only one thing will matter on that judgment day.
Will He find me in self righteous, filthy rags or
Clothed in His righteousness divine?
Will I stand before Him ashamed or
Bow before Him in humility,
Bringing glory to His Holy Name?
Only one thing is important today
To listen to His voice,
To walk in obedience to His will.

In a Little While

In a little while my Lord will come
In a little while to take me home
In a little while no fears, no tears
In a little while no sadness, all gladness
In a little while no more goodbyes
In my home beyond the skies.

And you now, therefore, have sorrow, but I will see you again and your heart will rejoice; and your joy no man takes from you John 16:22

The Last Flight

Hand in hand mom and I walked down the ramp to Flight 1280. Dad was being pushed in the wheelchair by the airline staff just ahead of us. Just before entering the plane dad was transferred to a special chair which fit in the aisle and enabled him to reach his assigned seat. Mom was seated by the window with myself in the middle. I thought, "Dad will surely sleep on the airplane". Talking slowly and clearly I did my best to explain to him that we were on our way to Texas. I wondered how much he comprehended. I held his hand to comfort him.

The plane take off was rapid. Some turbulance was in the air. In a short time we were at an altitude of 31,000 feet. Our ears hurt from the increased pressure. Dad was restless. Placing both hands on the back of the seat in front of us, he tried to stand up. I took a piece of paper and pen. Printing large letters, I explained that he must stay seated. We would soon be in Texas. My husband would meet us at the airport and take us home. I gave the paper and pencil to dad. Pushing the pencil with some effort he wrote, "I will try harder and it will go better".

My heart longed for dad to understand that he did not need to struggle to do the things he was no longer able to do. He had cared for me so many times when I was growing up; now I felt it a privilege to care for him. Yet, how difficult it must be for one to depend upon others. The flight attendant brought a snack of turkey sandwich, tomatoes and lettuce, carrot sticks and cookies . Dad was able to eat all except the carrot sticks. This was a good diversion which helped the time pass more quickly.

(Continued next page)

The plane stopped at Houston. We were glad that we could keep our seats in the plane without transferring to another plane to Dallas. Dad watched as other passengers left the plane. Reaching his hand into the aisle, he obviously was wondering what we were waitng for. We reminded him that the plane would soon take off again and we would be in Dallas shortly. The time went quickly from Houston to Dallas. Snacking on pretzels kept Dad's mind occupied. Mom was so courageous. When the two wearied travelers arrived in Dallas what a welcome sight it was to see my husband. Our dear friend and neighbor, David had come along with his roomy Buick. David was such help in transferring dad from the wheelchair into his car.

Three weeks later I am on Flight 1280 again, flying from Minneapolis to Dallas. Mom is again with me and my husband beside me. Our daughter, Sarah, is beside mom. Dad has taken another flight. His flight is much higher; he has reached his destination

Borne up on angel wings, above the clouds and sunset rise,

The way is sure; the Son of Man has gone before.

All earthly cares are left behind.

Heaven's gate is opened wide.

Welcomed home by angel hosts,

Dad has taken his final flight

(In memory of my father.)

List of Songs Which I Have Quoted from in My Book

Behind the Clouds by Carolyn R. Freeman

His Eye is on the Sparrow Words by Civilla D. Martin, Music by Charles H. Gabriel

God Is So Good African Folk Song

How Firm a Foundation, Words by George Keith Music attr.to Anne Steele

I Have Decided Words anonymous, Music Indian Folk Tune

If Jesus Goes with Me by C. Austin Miles

Jesus, I Am Resting, Resting by Jean Pigoutt

Jesus Loves Even Me by Philip P. Bliss

Jesus Will Outshine Them All by Gordon Jensen

Running Over by William Gardner Hunter

For more information about persecuted Christians around the world contact:

The Voice of the Martyrs

P O Box 443

Bartlesville, Oklahoma, 74005

Telephone – (918) 337-8015

Web site – www.persecution.com